Beginner's Guide to Selling Amazon Private Label (FBA)

The Secrets to Succeeding Selling Amazon

LAUNCH your first product and make Extra passive Income

A step-by-Step Guide for Beginners and Intermediate Sellers

Table of Contents

Introduction

Chapter 1: What Is Amazon FBA?

Chapter 2: Reasons Why You Should Sell On Amazon

Chapter 3: What Are Private Label Products?

Chapter 4: How To Research For The Types Of Products That You Are Going To Sell On Amazon

Chapter 5: How And Where To Find Manufacturers Or Suppliers Of Your Product

Chapter 6: Preparing Your Products For Sale

Chapter 7: Everything You Need To Know About Launching Your Products

Chapter 8: Strategies On How To Generate Your Initial Product Reviews

Chapter 9: How To Use As Leverage The Amazon Sponsored Products Feature

Chapter 10: Practical Tips On How To Attract More Customers For Your Amazon Products

Chapter 11: Common Pitfalls And Mistakes You Should Avoid When Selling On Amazon FBA

Chapter 12: How To Effectively Scale Your Amazon FBA Business

Conclusion

Introduction

"*You sell it, we ship it.*" That is the tagline for the Amazon FBA program. It perfectly encapsulates what the program is all about. In a lot of ways, the program has revolutionized how entrepreneurs market and distribute their goods online. Without a doubt, the program's biggest accomplishment to date is the fact that it has made it easier for sellers to bring their products closer to their target customers. Many of the technical aspects of handling and shipping goods are now taken over by Amazon itself. It means that there's less work for sellers. This is especially important for small sellers who don't have the resources to store and ship products on their own.

In this book, we are going to discuss the most important aspects of starting and growing an online business using the Amazon FBA program. It's not as complicated as you might think. There's a few technical steps that can be intimidating at first, but other than these, running an Amazon FBA business is similar to running an ordinary online business. You will soon get the hang of it to the point where you can run the entire operation with your eyes closed. Okay, that is probably an exaggeration but you get the point. Using the program gets easier as you learn more about how it works and how you can take advantage of its various features and functions.

The number one reason why a lot of aspiring online entrepreneurs fail on the Amazon FBA program is that they start blind. That is, they dive right into the platform without learning about it first. That is a pitfall you can avoid if you read this book in its entirety. This is why I've embarked on writing this book to serve as your guide in starting a business using the platform.

Is the Amazon FBA program for you? If you are a small or a medium-sized retailer and seller, the platform is definitely the perfect choice for you. If you are worried about the costs of operating an online business, Amazon basically takes nearly all of these costs away. This is the main reason why Amazon created the program in the first place. They want to offer a solution to the operational woes that besiege small and mid-sized online retailers and sellers. What the program does is handle the operational responsibility through their network of fulfillment centers. Even customer service is handled by them.

I specifically wrote this book to fill a knowledge gap. There's a dearth of comprehensive information and resources out there that target serious Amazon sellers. There's also a ton of information out there about the Amazon FBA program that are downright misleading or inaccurate. My goal is to make these errors right and offer compelling and accurate information on how to use the program. A lot of the information you are going to find in this book is taken from first-hand experience and from what I've learned from those who have been really successful in using the program.

In a nutshell, the Amazon FBA program is a platform you should definitely try if you are looking for a way to easily distribute your products to a global marketplace. But before you dive in, make sure that you read this book from the first chapter to the last. Good luck.

Chapter 1: What Is Amazon FBA?

FBA is an acronym that stands for Fulfillment by Amazon. It's basically an e-commerce program that Amazon specifically designed to cater to the thousands of online entrepreneurs who are clamoring to sell their goods within Amazon. However, Amazon is aware of the fact that there are already dozens of sites online where people can list and sell their goods. So the company needed to come up with something that would separate their e-commerce program from everyone else. So they came up with the idea of fulfillment centers. Sellers just have to ship their goods to these fulfillment centers and Amazon will handle the rest of the business. They store the goods and fulfill customer orders on behalf of the sellers.

The idea took off almost immediately. Thousands of online entrepreneurs are currently signed up with the Amazon FBA program and they rake in hundreds of millions of sales every year. The program has become one of Amazon's biggest revenue streams. With the program, Amazon accomplished two very important things. One, they welcomed with open arms third-party sellers. And two, they implemented efficient and long-term free shipping programs. These are the two most important reasons why online entrepreneurs are flocking to Amazon to sell their goods.

How Fulfillment by Amazon Works

How the program operates is quite simple. Let's say you have goods that you want to sell through the internet. You sign up with the Amazon FBA program and get your products ready by labelling and packaging them as per the policies and conditions put forth by the program. You then ship these products to Amazon's fulfillment centers. Amazon receives the packages and stores these in their warehouses. If a customer orders your product, Amazon picks the product from their shelves, packages it, and ships it to the location of the customer. Not only that, Amazon also handles customer inquiries on your behalf.

If that wasn't clear enough, here's the fulfillment process in steps:

1. <u>Seller ships his goods to Amazon's fulfillment centers.</u> Amazon has a lot of fulfillment centers so you send your items to the ones that are nearest you. Amazon accepts both new and used products. You also have the flexibility to decide how much goods you send on a month-to-month basis.

2. <u>Amazon stacks and stores the goods.</u> After receiving your goods in one of their fulfillment centers, Amazon takes the responsibility of cataloguing and storing the goods. Your products are safe and sound in their network of fulfillment centers.

3. <u>A customer orders the product.</u> If you have properly completed your Amazon Seller's account, your products should be listed on Amazon.com or on other sales channels associated with the company's fulfillment program.

4. <u>Amazon fulfills the customer's order by packing and shipping it to his address.</u> After receiving the customer order, Amazon fulfills it by picking, packaging, labelling, and shipping the product to its final destination. Of course, there are fulfillment fees that come with the process. This is how Amazon makes money from the program. The fulfillment fees you pay depend on various factors including the category of the item, its product size tier, and its selling price. You can learn more about these fees and other related costs by visiting Amazon's Pricing Page.

5. Amazon addresses customer questions and inquiries. Customer service is handled by Amazon's expansive and world-class team of customer support professionals. These professionals handle customer issues such as inquiries, refunds, and product returns.

Of course, this is just an overview of the whole process. It's merely a framework. Each step comes with what are called sub-steps. Don't worry, all of these will be thoroughly discussed in the succeeding chapters. We are going to go over the process from start to finish.

Scaling Your Amazon FBA Business

One of the most important benefits of the FBA business model is how easy it is to scale your operations. Keep in mind that unlike a traditional retail operation, you don't need space to store expanding inventory. You also don't need to hire additional customer service representatives. Storage and customer support are handled by Amazon itself. This means that if you scale your business by adding more products, the additional costs in your account are minimal. You can add as many products as you want. Aside from attracting more customers, adding more goods in your listing is the most effective way to scale your operations.

The Amazon FBA Program Saves You a Lot of Time

If you look at the business model of the program, you will realize that Amazon is basically running the business for you. They store your products, they pack them, they respond to customer orders, and they ship the items to customers. Technically speaking, you are merely a supplier. You bring the products to Amazon and Amazon sells the products on your behalf. Needless to say, you save a lot of valuable time from the simple fact that most of the processes are handled by Amazon. You don't have to burden yourself with fulfilling orders and shipping products to customers. You don't even deal with customers who are not satisfied with your products.

It's not that difficult to see why thousands are gravitating towards the Amazon FBA program. Even established online entrepreneurs who are already making money from their own operations are slowly transitioning to the Amazon FBA program. This benefits them in two major ways. One, they can significantly cut down their operational and overhead costs. And two, they can use Amazon's influence and popularity as leverage to reach more customers.

Using FBA and Having the Prime Badge

Another great feature of selling goods through the Amazon FBA program is that FBA products are eligible for Amazon Prime. What difference does this make? Well, what if I told you that there are more than 30 million Amazon Prime users. That's right. These are additional customers for you on top of regular Amazon shoppers. Prime subscribers are more valuable than regular Amazon users because they spend more and shop more through Amazon. Furthermore, they tend to prefer purchasing Prime-eligible products. So sometimes, when they search for goods on Amazon, they filter the results so that these will only show Prime-eligible items.

Quick note: *Prime is a membership program wherein customers get free two-day shipping for only $99 per year. It was first introduced by Amazon to customers back in 2007. If a customer orders a product, the shipping is free and the product arrives at his doorstep within 1 to 2 days. Members also have access to a search sorting feature, which enables them to sort Prime Offers from Super Saver Shipping.*

As a seller, it's difficult to turn down the features and benefits being offered by the Amazon FBA program. The program's business model is second to none. Amazon is the only online marketplace offering the model and it would be a huge mistake if you don't take on the opportunity. If you want to sell more products in a larger marketplace and at lower costs, the Amazon FBA program is the perfect platform for you.

Chapter 2: Reasons Why You Should Sell On Amazon

There are dozens of marketplaces online where you can sell your products, so why should you choose Amazon? It's important that I tell you right now that there's absolutely no reason why you should only focus your selling efforts on Amazon. There's this common misconception among new online sellers that if you are going to sell on Amazon, you should only sell on Amazon; that you should completely ignore all the other online marketplaces available out there.

My point here is that you can sell on Amazon and sell on other platforms. That's what a lot of other online entrepreneurs do and they are reaping the rewards. More platforms to use means more potential customers for your products. So you need to dispel that myth that Amazon should be the one and only marketplace you use. With that out of the way, let us now take a look into some of the most important reasons why you should be selling on Amazon.

1. Online commerce is growing at a very fast pace. At the forefront of this rapid expansion are major online marketplaces like Amazon. Amazon is the biggest brand as far as online commerce is concerned. When people talk about online commerce, they talk about Amazon. When people talk about purchasing goods online, they talk about Amazon. Online commerce will continue to grow and it is showing zero signs of slowing down. Needless to say, if you want a piece of the action, now is the time to take your chance. And you should definitely take your chance through Amazon.

2. Traffic going into Amazon has much higher conversion rates compared to other platforms. Amazon is a shopping site so most of the people arriving in its pages are looking to purchase something. It doesn't matter if people arrive on Amazon from search engines, from social media sites, from forums, or from referrals in blogs and websites. They are usually interested in buying goods. If someone is viewing your listing on Amazon, it means that person is interested in buying what you are offering.

3. Amazon has a very effective product recommendation system. When you view a product listing on Amazon, you will notice that the page also contains several recommendations for similar and relevant products. This is very important to you as a seller in the platform. The recommendations page is basically free promotion and advertising for your products. Your product will be featured as a recommended item in listings of products that are similar or relevant to your product. For example, if you are selling an ebook about real estate, your ebook will be showing up as a recommended book in listings of books about real estate. Amazon grew so fast because of their powerful recommendations system.

4. Amazon offers a more secure platform for online sellers. One of the biggest problems with other online marketplaces is that they often have security issues. Accounts of sellers get hacked and their earnings stolen. Opportunistic buyers can easily manipulate the refund and return policies to get their money back without returning the items delivered to them. Sellers sometimes see their goods get lost. These are very serious problems and Amazon has found ways to have them under control.

5. Amazon provides you with tools and resources to help you sell more of your products. These include guides, tutorials, and articles on how to get the most of the platform's features and functions. Amazon also has its own seller forums where you can connect and engage with other sellers. These forums are free and there's a ton of information you can learn from the threads there. You can ask questions from sellers who are more successful than you. These community forums were basically set up by Amazon so that you can all learn from each other.

6. Products listed in Amazon FBA have access to Amazon Prime subscribers. This also means that your products are eligible for free shipping. Free shipping is a huge incentive. Let's take you as example. How many times have you purchased a product because the seller is offering free shipping? Probably more times than you can count. I think I've already mentioned earlier the fact that Amazon Prime has around 50 million members. And these members spend more money on Amazon compared to regular members.

7. Selling on Amazon will cost you less. It is definitely more cost-effective to sell your products through the Amazon FBA program compared to getting the services of a third-party dropshipper. Outsourcing through other third parties comes with a lot of extra expenses and overhead costs. If you use the Amazon FBA program, all you need to do is send the products to Amazon's fulfillment centers. Your expenses and costs will be concentrated on this process. There are no extra costs and hidden fees.

8. It is easy to scale your operations. There are two major strategies on how to quickly expand your business on Amazon. One, just add more products to your listings. And two, double or triple your volume. These are very easy to do on the platform for the simple fact that you just have to ship your goods to Amazon's fulfillment centers. You don't have to do anything else, remember? Amazon handles orders, packaging, shipping, and even customer service. So even if you add more products or increase your volume, the additional burden will still be handled by Amazon.

In short, if you plan on selling goods online without building your own market platform, Amazon is your best option. If you have the products in your hand, you are good to go. Ship the goods to Amazon's fulfillment centers and the retail giant will take care of the rest. It sounds too good to be true but that's really how the process works. Amazon basically takes over most of the burden for you.

Chapter 3: What Are Private Label Products?

Here's the simplest definition I can offer you for private label products. These are simply goods created by one company that can be branded and sold by another company. In other words, you don't create or manufacture the products. You simply get the products from another company, rebrand the products, put your labels on them, and sell them as if you created them yourself.

Essentially, what you do is look for generic products that can be sold on Amazon, create your own packaging and labels for these products, then list them for sale on Amazon. That's the whole framework of the business model.

In creating a private label business, there are three parties involved. The first one is the manufacturer or supplier of the products. This is the party that does the dirty work of designing and creating the products. The second party is you. You are the retailer who gets the products from the manufacturer. You create your own packaging, labels, and logos for the products to make them your own. You put your stamp and branding on them. The third party is the marketplace or platform where you are going to sell the goods. In this case, that third party would be Amazon.

Selling private label products is very similar to retail arbitrage. The only difference is that you don't sell the products as is. You need to rebrand the products to make them your own. In retail arbitrage, you simply buy products complete with logos, labels, and the markings of a brand. You just resell them for a profit. In private labelling, you need to go the extra distance by putting your own labels and logos on the products you sell.

One of the benefits of selling private label products is that you can do almost everything through your laptop. For example, you can get in touch with a manufacturer or supplier in China. Have them manufacture your products. Have them put your logos and labels on the products as well. And last but not the least, you can instruct them to ship the labelled products directly to Amazon's fulfillment centers. This means that you don't even handle the inventory. Everything is done online.

However, if you want to have complete control over the quality of the products you are selling, we recommend that you have the products shipped to you first before you have them shipped to the fulfillment centers. This way, you can check if the products are up to the quality and standard you expected.

Chapter 4: How To Research For The Types Of Products That You Are Going To Sell On Amazon

This is without a doubt the most important step in starting a business on the Amazon FBA program. Everything will be dependent on how well you perform in this step. As you should know, Amazon is the biggest marketplace online. Almost anything that you can think of is being sold on the site. Let's perform a quick exercise. Off the top of your head, think of a really absurd product. Then do a quick search for it on the Amazon website. I bet your search will generate dozens if not hundreds of product listings. My point here is that literally everything under the sun is being sold on Amazon.

This brings me to my next point which is "competition". Because of the immense number of goods being offered for sale on Amazon, the competition among sellers is just as immense. You may have a good product in your hands but if you are up against cutthroat competition, then you have very little chance in moving forward. This is why it's important that you do your research first before you start selling on Amazon. You need to look for products that have a market but aren't too competitive. To simplify things, your product should meet two factors:

1. There's a demand for it.
2. Only a few people are selling it on Amazon.

You have to keep in mind that not all products can be sold via the Amazon FBA program. There are goods that are simply too cumbersome to sell on the platform. There are certain attributes that you should look for in a product that makes it a viable Amazon FBA item. The most important of such attributes are as follows.

a. It has to be lightweight and small. Remember that you will be shipping the items to one of Amazon's fulfillment centers. The bigger and heavier the items are, the more expenses you will spend on shipping and storage. The general rule is that your product should be able to fit snugly into a flat-rate box. It should not weigh more than one or two pounds.

b. It should be unregulated. Or it could be regulated but the rules are not that stringent. The problem in selling regulated products like batteries, toys, and food is that they come with red tape which makes them hard to sell because you need to go through a lot of paperwork and certifications. For example, if you are going to sell toys for children, you have to acquire several approvals and certifications to prove that your toys do not pose health hazards to kids.

c. The products should be non-seasonal. This basically means that you can sell the products in any season. It doesn't matter if it's January or July or December. Demand for the product should be all year round. Examples of seasonal products are Christmas lights, Valentine's Day cards, Halloween costumes. These are products that you should avoid because demand for them are very seasonal.

d. The products should be uncomplicated. You can just ship them to the fulfillment centers with little worries. A mouse pad is a good example of an uncomplicated product. Electronic gadgets are examples of complicated products. Electronics may be fun to sell but they come with a ton of headaches and customer service issues. They have so many moving parts. What if a customer wants to replace a part? What if the customer can't find the appropriate batteries for it? Keep in mind that you are selling dozens if not hundreds of these products. Imagine if a good number of your customers find issues with the products. You will be inundated with dozens of emails and inquiries.

To help you with your research, here are some very ***practical tips on how to look for good products to sell*** through the Amazon FBA program:

1. Dig through the departments and sub-categories within Amazon to look for new products and new releases. Your first step in your product research should be within the Amazon website itself. Browse through the site's various departments, categories, and sub-categories. You can get dozens of product ideas by scrolling through the listings. Keep notes on the products that catch your attention. Jot them down on a pad paper so that you can get back on them later on for more in-depth research. The great thing about product listings within Amazon's departments and categories is that you can sort the products using various criteria like popularity, price range, date of release, and average reviews. Looking into these information can help you decide if it's worth it to pursue a particular product or not.

2. Look into what other people are selling through the Amazon FBA program. This is very easy to do. It's the same as what we have discussed above in number one but you focus on products that are specifically being sold by entrepreneurs enrolled in the FBA program. You can determine which products are getting a lot of sales based on the number of reviews they get and how well they rank in the search results. Look at these products, look at the people selling them, and try to understand why they are very successful in the platform. Your main objective here is to identify the things that they are doing right and see if you can replicate them.

3. Take advantage of Jungle Scout. This is an extension for the Chrome browser which makes it very easy for you to perform product research on Amazon. All you have to do is do a query on Amazon for a particular product idea. When the search results finish loading, you simply click on the Jungle Scout button on the right side of your browser's address bar. The extension will provide you with valuable information about the product such as average reviews per product, average monthly sales, and price fluctuations. Of course, you can only use the Jungle Scout extension if you purchased and downloaded it. Yes, it comes with a price but it's completely worth it.

4. Get ideas from Google Trends. This is a free service by Google which shows you the topics and queries that are very popular among users of the search engine. The service shows you what topics are trending, what topics are increasing in popularity, what topics are losing steam. These are usually shown alongside simple graphs so that you can easily understand and sometimes predict the direction of a trend. These trends can help you brainstorm for product ideas. For example, if the topic healthy food is trending, this means you need to think about products that might fulfill the needs of people who are searching for information about healthy food products.

5. Stay away from departments and categories on Amazon that are dominated by global brands. It's usually a waste of time trying to compete with the big brands. They have established themselves on Amazon and often times, you can't compete with them when it comes to price no matter how good your products are. So if you are doing product research on Amazon and you learn that big companies are already selling the products you have in mind, you should move on and look for other ideas.

6. Look for evergreen products. Evergreen is a term used to describe products that are in demand no matter the time of the year. It basically means that the product is not seasonal. People are buying it from January to December. Good examples of evergreen products are common household items, standard apparel like shirts and jeans, books, art supplies, etc. These are goods that are in demand throughout the year. If you want to run an Amazon FBA business that's profitable all year round, then you should only sell evergreen products.

7. Get product ideas using a keyword research tool. A keyword research tool is an online application that enables you to analyze sets and groups of keywords and keyword phrases. It's a powerful way to look for suggestions related to your product idea. For example, let's say that you plan on selling leather sandals on Amazon FBA. Using a keyword research tool, you can find many keywords that are relevant to the term "leather sandals". You might come across relevant keywords like "leather sandals for children", "leather hiking sandals", "leather house sandals", or "leather slippers". You may not eventually use these additional keywords but they can provide you with really good product ideas that you can pursue in your next project or next online campaign.

8. Find products that you can sell at higher margins. Selling a $2 toy at $5 is better than selling a $300 camera at $301. At first glance, it seems like selling a $300 camera is more lucrative and more profitable than selling a $2 toy. But if you look at the revenue per item, the toy earned $3 while the camera earned only $1. What I am trying to say here is that you should look for low-cost products that you can resell at high margins. Don't make the mistake of assuming that higher-priced items will net you more profits.

9. Do product research in other online marketplaces like eBay or Clickbank. Or you can browse the websites of major retailers like Walmart and Target to see what types of products are selling like hotcakes in their platforms. You go through the sites the way you go through Amazon. Look at the popular products. Look at what the biggest sellers are doing. Find out which products are getting the most reviews. Crunch through the information and see if you can sell the same products on Amazon.

In using these strategies in product research, you should be able to come up with the right products for your FBA business. Take your time with your research. Don't rush because rushing is often the culprit behind ill-planned products. You don't have to use all of the research strategies I have discussed in this chapter. Just use the ones that work well for your business and niche.

Chapter 5: How And Where To Find Manufacturers Or Suppliers Of Your Product

Okay, so you have done your product research and you've made up your mind when it comes to the types of products you want to promote and sell. You are not going to make these products yourself so you need to look for suppliers and manufacturers. This will require another round of researching and snooping from you. You need to look for reliable and reputable suppliers. You also take the time to observe what your direct competitors are doing. For example, you should know where they are getting their products and how are they paying for these products. If they are successful in what they are doing, then they are doing something right. Maybe you can replicate that success.

One of the best and most popular marketplaces for dropshippers and Amazon FBA program merchants is Alibaba. If you are not that familiar with Alibaba and how it works, just think of it as the Amazon of China. It's a company that makes it very easy for you to purchase goods wholesale or in bulk. Majority of the merchants within the Alibaba platform are suppliers and manufacturers. This makes the platform the perfect option for dropshippers and for sellers using the Amazon FBA program.

How to Use Alibaba to Look for Product Suppliers and Manufacturers
The very first thing you should do is create a buyer's account on Alibaba. There are basically two types of accounts on the platform: buyer accounts and seller accounts. Once you have completed your account, you can start browsing through products in the site using the search function. The platform's product database is very similar to that of Amazon. If you make a search, listings of

relevant and related products will populate the search results. You can click on individual listings to get more information about the products.

If you are interested in a particular product, all you have to do is message the supplier or manufacturer. You request for additional information that may not be available in the original listing. For example, you might want to know the unit price for a product if you are going to buy 1000 pieces of the products. Or how many of the goods can they produce within a specific time period. What are the payment terms and what payment options are available to you? Can you customize the products? These are the most important questions you need to ask the supplier and manufacturer.

And yes, before I forget, you should also ask if you can have a sample of the product shipped to your address so that you can check the goods for yourself. Don't forget to ask how much it would cost to have the sample product shipped to your address. Legit and reliable suppliers or manufacturers are usually more than willing to send in samples of their goods. Sometimes, they send these samples for free. That is you don't have to pay anything for them. These are the types of suppliers that you should be working with because they are really serious about their business and the potential partnership they will have with you.

Don't just reach out to a few suppliers and manufacturers on Alibaba. Always keep your options open. Chances are there are dozens of suppliers and manufacturers selling the products that you have in mind. You must take the time to reach out to several suppliers and weigh their offers against each other. Your goal is to find the supplier who can provide you the best products at the least cost. Always make sure to request or order sample products from the supplier. If a supplier is reluctant in providing you with a sample, then something is amiss. Either he is not that confident about the quality of his product or he is a scammer. It's worth mentioning here that Alibaba has its own fair share of scammers and con artists. These are people who pose as sellers and manufacturers only to suddenly disappear once the payment for your orders has gone through to them.

Other Wholesale Suppliers in China Aside from Alibaba

Let's face it, China is still your best option when it comes to sourcing products for your Amazon FBA business. Not only do you have access to cheap products, you also have tons of suppliers to choose from. If because of some reason you can't use Alibaba as your source, don't worry because you have several other options. These would include the following platforms:

1. AliExpress - This is actually a subsidiary of Alibaba, which means most of the merchants in the platform are sub-suppliers. They may not have an inventory listing that is as big as that of Alibaba but the company is still a great option for your business.
2. Chinabrands - This online marketplace offers its services to more than 200 countries globally. They have more than half a million products in their inventory. The company also has a rewards program that enables loyal customers to earn points and use such points to pay for future purchases at discounted prices.
3. DHgate - Think of this marketplace as the younger brother of Alibaba. It offers almost the same products as those available on Alibaba. It's possible that a lot of the merchants in Alibaba have also built accounts on DHgate. Regardless of this possibility, DHgate is still a nice place to look for products to sell in your Amazon FBA business. They have dozens of categories for their selections.
4. Global Sources - This company is not as big as the others mentioned above but it makes up with high-quality services and a range of good products. One of the great things about this

company is that they perform credit checks, capability assessments, and verifications for all their suppliers. For these reasons, Global Sources is known for their reliable suppliers and higher quality products.

5. Bangood - Two of the biggest selling points of Bangood is that they offer low cost shipping and fast product delivery. Having been established in 2006, Bangood has been around for quite a while so they know the business well, and they have evolved through the years. They started out selling computers and technology products, but they were able to expand their product line. Now, they carry inventories of products that range from clothing and apparel to sports and outdoor gear.

What If You Want to Deal with Suppliers Within the United States?

Maybe you would want to get your products from suppliers within the United States. That's a noble idea because you will be supporting suppliers and manufacturers within the country. However, you have to understand that products from within the United States are much more expensive compared to products you can get from other countries like China or India. For example, a product that you can get for $1 from China can cost you $10 in the United States. This is not an exaggeration. There's a reason why majority of sellers using the Amazon FBA program get their products overseas.

Anyway, if you want to source your products from within the US, the good news is that you have several platforms to choose from. The best of these marketplaces include the following:

1. Orange Shine - If you are planning to sell fashion products through the Amazon FBA program, then Orange Shine is the perfect wholesale supplier for you. Orange Shine is an online wholesale marketplace that specializes in clothing, shoes, bags, jewelry, and fashion accessories. Orange Shine is home to hundreds of brands and manufacturers in the fashion industry.

2. Worldwide Brands - This is the biggest wholesale supplier directory in the US. This alone is enough reason to use the platform when looking for product suppliers. They have an extensive directory of verified and certified suppliers. They have a refund policy and their membership program lasts for life. This means you only pay a one-time fee and you will become a member for life.

3. Wholesale Central - Based in the state of Connecticut, Wholesale Central is another great alternative for those looking for a US-based wholesale supplier. The company has been around since 1996 so you know they have a sustainable and credible business environment. The website is also free to use, although there's a premium service if you want to access their premium offers. The site also contains a lot of helpful tools that connect wholesale suppliers with interested retailers.

4. SaleHoo - Although this is a New Zealand company, they have a lot of US suppliers in their directory. To be able to use SaleHoo, you need to register and create an account, which will cost you $67. Don't worry, that amount is good for one year. This means you are paying less than $10 a month for their awesome services. There are over 1000 suppliers in SaleHoo. This may seem like a drop in the bucket but there's a reason why SaleHoo only partners with few suppliers. They assess every supplier who wants to be on their directory.

5. Megagoods - This is a niche directory because they specialize in working with suppliers who sell consumer electronics and video game products. Here's a quick overview of some of the products being sold on the site: watches, digital clocks, Bluetooth products, car security items, digital cameras, DVD players, speakers, video cameras, home theaters, headphones, etc. So if you are planning to sell electronic products and video games on Amazon, Megagoods is a great place to look for products.

Negotiating with Suppliers and Manufacturers

Just because a supplier lists a product at $5 per unit doesn't mean that's the amount you are going to pay for it. You should learn how to haggle and renegotiate the prices. Most suppliers and manufacturers are more than willing to drive down their prices as long as the deal is reasonable. Don't settle for what is listed as prices for the products. Many suppliers and manufacturers purposely put high price tags on their goods with the anticipation that potential clients will be negotiating for lower prices.

There are two things that you can put into the table to entice the supplier to lower down his prices. One, you promise that you will be ordering regularly from him. This one is hard to refuse on the part of the supplier because you are presenting yourself as a potential repeat customer. Two, you will be ordering the goods in bulk. This means that whatever the supplier loses in the lowered prices, he will get it back because of the sheer volume of goods you are purchasing. These are two offers that any sane supplier or manufacturer will find difficult to turn down.

My point here is that you have to be a good negotiator if you want to be successful selling products using the Amazon FBA program. You will always be negotiating with suppliers and manufacturers. You will always be looking for ways on how to drive down the prices you have to pay for the goods you are selling.

To summarize things, you have a lot of options when it comes to where you should get the products that you are going to sell through the Amazon FBA program. Like most entrepreneurs using the program, your first choice will always be suppliers and manufacturers who are based in China. They have the most affordable products that you can purchase in bulk. Of course, if for some reason you don't want to source your products from China, you can always get in touch with suppliers and manufacturers that are based within the United States. But you have to keep in mind that products from US suppliers and manufacturers are often way more expensive compared to their Chinese counterparts.

Chapter 6: Preparing Your Products For Sale

This is a very important step in the Amazon FBA process. You need to make sure that you have prepared your products properly before these are shipped to a fulfillment center. Some products require more preparation than others, so it's necessary that you read Amazon's policies and instructions on how you should prepare and send your products to their fulfillment centers. Through its Seller Central resource page, Amazon provides you with all the information you need in preparing your products for their fulfillment centers. I highly suggest that you completely read the resources before proceeding.

Before preparing your products for shipment, make sure that you have browsed through Amazon's FBA product restrictions and shipping and routing requirements. Amazon is very specific in identifying what products are suitable for their fulfillment process and which products they don't accept in the program.

You have to understand that Amazon is very strict in enforcing their rules and policies on products that are sent to them via the FBA program. If you fail to comply with their requirements, they can either refuse, return, or even dispose the products you send to them. Not only that, they can refuse and block shipments from you in the future. For these reasons, you should go over Amazon's product requirements and restrictions several times before you start preparing your products for shipment.

Below is a quick overview of Amazon's rules and policies on restricted products, products and categories requiring approval, and restricted products.

Here's a list of restricted products. This doesn't necessarily mean that you can't sell these on Amazon or on the FBA program. It's just that these are subjected to a lot more approvals and requirements. If you are planning to sell any of these products, you should visit Amazon's restricted products page and read Amazon's additional requirements and policies for these particular goods.

1. Alcohol
2. Fine art
3. Automotive and powersports products
4. Cosmetics, skin care products, and hair care products
5. Dietary supplements
6. Electronics
7. Export controls
8. Chilled and frozen foods
9. Hazardous and dangerous items such as rechargeable batteries and refrigerants
10. Jewelry and precious gems
11. Lighting products
12. Medical devices and accessories
13. Organic products
14. Plants, seeds, and other plant products
15. Recalled products
16. Sex and sensuality products
17. Surveillance equipment
18. Warranties, contracts, guarantees, and service plans

19. Animals and animal-related products

20. Art under home decor

21. Composite wooden products

22. Currency, gift cards, coins, and cash equivalents

23. Drugs and drug paraphernalia

24. Weapons, explosives, and related items

25. Food and beverage

26. Lottery and gambling products

27. Human parts and burial artifacts

28. Laser products

29. Lock picking and other types of theft devices

30. Controversial and offensive materials

31. Pesticides and pesticide devices

32. Stamps and postage meters

33. Recycled electronics and gadgets

34. Periodicals and subscriptions

35. Tobacco and tobacco-related products

36. Video game bundles without pre-approval from Amazon

37. Real property or real estate

38. Event tickets

39. Coupons

40. Domain names

Products and categories that require approval:

1. Holiday selling guidelines in toys and games

2. Video, DVD, and Blu-ray

3. Streaming Media Players

4. Amazon Watch Warranty FAQs

5. Collectible Coins

Now that you know which products and categories are suitable or not suitable for the Amazon FBA program, let's now proceed to the actual process of preparing the products for shipment to Amazon's fulfillment centers. Below is a quick guide on how you should go about with the process.

General Packaging Requirements

1. Here's something you need to understand. Amazon can return, refuse, or repackage any item that reaches their fulfillment centers if it's inadequate or it wasn't compliant with the Amazon FBA's requirements. You will be charged for the expenses incurred in these processes. To avoid these extra costs, see to it that you adhere to all the packaging requirements and rules.

2. If you are going to use a FNSKU (Fulfillment Network Stock Keeping Unit) on a unit of product, it should correspond to a unique item. A product unit with a different size, a different color, or a different type should also have a different and unique FNSKU. If you don't do this properly, a lot of problems and confusion can ensue when you ship your products to Amazon.

3. Each unit of product you ship should contain a scannable label or barcode. This code should be located outside of the packaging box. The code should also come with the corresponding numbers that can be read by both humans and by a barcode reader. Remember, this barcode

and label should be on the box of each product unit. If you are sending products in bulk, see to it that each item in the shipment has its own barcode and label.

4. Comply with Amazon's barcode requirements. There are two types of barcodes that you can use for your products. You can use manufacturer barcodes (i.e. ISBN, JAN, EAN, UPC, and GCID). Or you can make use of Amazon's own barcodes. Here's how it works. If your products contain the manufacturer's barcodes, then these are the barcodes you are going to use for your unit products. In the absence of these manufacturer barcodes, you have to make do with Amazon barcodes (FNSKU).

How do you get Amazon barcodes? You have two options. One, you get the codes, print them out, and stick them to your products yourself. Most sellers on Amazon use this option. If you don't have the time to do this yourself, Amazon can do it for you for a fee. Yes, Amazon prints and applies the barcodes and charges you on a per unit basis. Amazon has a lot of resources including tutorial videos on how these barcodes work. I highly suggest that you go through these videos and tutorials. You can access these resources on the Help section of the Amazon Seller Central page.

5. If there are other barcodes in the product packaging that are still scannable, remove them or cover them so that only the manufacturer's barcodes are eligible. To render the barcodes unscannable, you can cover it with a felt-tip marker or run an opaque tape over it. This is to avoid the risk that the wrong barcode is read by Amazon's scanners during the receiving process.

6. For products with loose and detachable parts, see to it that they are securely taped and attached to each other. For instance, if you are selling a bag with detachable accessories, make

sure that these aren't separated during transit and shipment. You don't want to be dealing with angry customers who bought your products with missing parts and accessories. Amazon directly states that they don't accept products that they have to assemble themselves. The best way to secure your items with detachable parts is to put them in bags or secure them with non-adhesive bands and tapes.

7. If you are selling sets of products, you should clearly identify in the packaging that the items are to be sold as sets. You have to let Amazon's fulfillment centers know that the items are to be received and sold to customers as sets. You can do this by simply creating labels that contain any of the following phrases: "sold as set", "this is a set", and "ready to ship as a set". You can also add a label that says "do not separate". It's always best to seal your sets to avoid any confusion.

8. If you are selling product units in boxes, these should be in boxes with six sides. These will likely be stacked in Amazon's storage rooms so make sure that the boxes are made of tough materials. They shouldn't collapse easily to pressure from the sides or from above. For boxes that have openings or perforations on the sides, they should pass a drop test. Drop the item from three feet on one side and then on a corner. Passing the drop test means the box didn't suffer from major damage due to the fall.

9. If you are using poly bags as packaging for your items, don't forget to provide suffocation warnings in the bags. The warning can either be printed on the bag or attached through a tag or label. Amazon is very serious about this. If your items don't have suffocation warnings, Amazon might refuse or return the products to you so that you can rebag them or add the necessary warnings. Furthermore, Amazon requires that the bags should be transparent and completely sealed.

10. If you are packing several product units in a pack, each unit in the pack must have a matching SKU. You should also see to it that every pack contains the same number of products. For example, if you ship a pack containing 15 units, all the other packs you ship should contain the same number of units. You can't send a pack of 15 units and then send another pack with 20 units. It's worth mentioning here that Amazon imposes a maximum number of units that can be contained in a pack. The limit per pack is 150 units.

11. For products with expiration dates, you are required to print the expiration date using a font size of 36-points or higher. The expiration dates should be printed on the individual units. Just because the expiration date is printed on the main box doesn't mean you shouldn't print the dates on the individual products. It's best to use stickers for the expiration dates.

12. If you are shipping your products in a pallet, Amazon requires that you put at least four labels on the pallet. One label should be visible at the center of the pallet. This helps you in meeting the label requirements being imposed by Amazon. Each pallet must be properly identified with the correct shipment ID labels.

13. Use at least two inches of cushioning between each of the items you are shipping. This is to ensure that none of your products get damaged during transit. There should also be enough cushioning on the sides of the boxes and pallets you are using to protect the items against bumps and falls. After packing your items, try shaking the box or package if there's too much room inside the box. If the items inside are shaking too much, this means you haven't packed them properly. They are very susceptible to damage during falls and bumps in transit.

14. When shipping cloth, fabric, and textiles, these can be easily damaged by humidity and dust. Thus Amazon requires that you place the items in boxes, shrink wraps, or poly bags. The wrappings should also be properly marked with suffocation warning labels. Clothing items can be bulky, so one trick you can follow is to fold the item to the smallest possible size before putting it into its box or packaging. Amazon specifically names boxes, cardboard footprints, labels, shrink wraps, and poly bags as their permitted packaging materials.

15. When shipping items that contain liquids, you need to package and secure them in a way that the liquids won't either break through or leak through the container. First of all, the item should be able to pass a three-foot drop test. Look for a hard surface, hover the item that's already packaged three feet high above the surface, then drop it to the surface. The product inside shouldn't suffer from any damage or leakage. This means that the package has passed the three-foot drop test. Another important thing you should check is that the product should have a double seal or a safety seal.

Where to Get Amazon Packaging Supplies

If there's something you should have learned about the product preparation requirements and guidelines that were discussed above, it's the fact that Amazon is rather specific when it comes to the materials you should use in packing, preparing, and shipping your products. The good news is that you can purchase most if not all of these packaging materials from Amazon itself. These include bubble packs, stretch wraps, shrink wraps, boxes, pallets, and poly bags.

You need to be very careful in packing, preparing, and shipping your products to Amazon's fulfillment centers to avoid unnecessary problems down the road. Not adhering to the requirements and guidelines can lead to a lot of problems that will eventually be very expensive to fix. Remember that you will be handling the costs and expenses associated with improperly prepared products.

For example, if you used the wrong packaging materials for a batch of products you shipped, Amazon might ship the items back to you. And you have to pay for the expenses the company incurred in shipping the goods back to you. You need to repack the products all over again using the prescribed materials. This means you will be doubling the costs and expenses of packing and shipping the items. In a nutshell, try to get the packaging and preparations right the first time to avoid doubling your shipping expenses.

Chapter 7: Everything You Need To Know About Launching Your Products

It's very important that we clearly define what we mean when we talk about launching a product in the context of the Amazon FBA program. You see, launching a product on Amazon may be very different as opposed to launching a product in a standard online business. Amazon has a unique business model. It basically means that launching a product in it is different from say, launching a product in your own stand-alone online store. Launching a product through the Amazon FBA program means preparing the goods, creating listings for them on Amazon, and making them available for purchase online. If a product is now in Amazon's inventory and viewable by potential customers, it means the product has been launched.

Creating a Listing on Amazon

Before preparing, packaging, and shipping your products to fulfillment centers, Amazon suggests that you create your product listings first. Don't worry, your listings won't show up on Amazon until the fulfillment center has received your shipment. There are two ways on how you can create a product listing through the FBA program depending on the number of products you want to list down. You can either add one product at a time or you can list products in bulk. As always, see to it that you follow all the FBA listing requirements when you enter the details about your products. The information in your listings should match the information contained in the labels and packaging of the products you are shipping.

1. Adding products one at a time. To create an individual listing, you use the Add a Product tool that is available when you click on the dropdown menu of the Inventory tab in your Amazon

Seller Account. Just follow the instructions from the tool. However, before you start creating the listing, make sure that you have the following information:

- Product details: These include information such as the name of the product, a short description, images of the product, brand (if any), and the category where it belongs to. These information provide the buyer with a clearer understanding of the product and what it can do for him/her. This is also where you highlight the main features of the product.
- Details of your offer: These details include the price of the product, its current condition (i.e. used or new), shipping choices, and quantities (i.e. 4 packets in one box). The information here aren't necessarily set on stone. You can update them whenever you want. For example, if you want to change the discount offer from 10% to 20%, you can do so by editing the details in this section.
- Product identifier: Nearly all products that can be listed on Amazon has an identification code that is unique to the product. Examples of such codes are ISBN, JAN, EAN, and UPC. These identification codes help in ensuring that the information associated with the listed product are as accurate as possible.
- Search terms and keywords: Using relevant keywords is very important in creating your listings because they help customers in finding your products. When you brainstorm for keywords, think of what your target customers might be using when they search for your products online. When choosing your keywords, don't use stop words (a, and, by), don't use brand names, don't use punctuations, and don't repeat words. Furthermore, try using variations of the keywords like synonyms, abbreviations, and alternative names.

2. Adding products in bulk. This is the way to go if you have a lot of products to create listings for. Instead of creating the listings individually, you can just make use of a flat file to upload the necessary information about your products. Amazon provides you with the templates that you can use for your file uploads. These templates are designed for specific categories so make sure that you download the templates that match the category of your products. You can easily download these templates from within your Amazon Seller Account.

These are merely templates, which means you still have to go over the product listings to change details if necessary. Unlike creating individual listings, using a template means the same information you entered into the template will be applied to all the listings. So it's still necessary to go over the listings in the event that there are variations in your pricing for certain products.

I'll have to remind you once again that all the information and resources you need to create product listings through the FBA program are available on the Amazon Seller page. There are detailed articles, guides, and even tutorial videos that show you all the steps you need to take in creating your product listings. What we have discussed in this particular chapter is just a framework of the necessary steps you need to take.

After creating your listings, preparing your products, and shipping them to the fulfillment centers, what's next? Well, first of all, you need to wait a bit for your product listings to go live on the Amazon website. When you finish creating a listing, this doesn't mean that the listing will automatically be available on Amazon. The product listing will only show up when your product shipments are received by one of Amazon's fulfilment centers. Only then will your product listings go live on Amazon.

It can take a few days or even up to a week for the shipment to be received by a fulfillment center and for your product listings to be activated. In the meantime, you should be busy setting up your marketing plans on how to maximize the number of people who will learn about your newly listed products. You should be creating buzz about your products. There's also the marketing strategy called pre-selling which basically involves reaching out to potential customers and attempting to sell the products in advance. This way, when the products finally become available for purchase, you have customers ready to get their hands on the product.

Creating Your Marketing Gameplan

A lot of new sellers on Amazon make the mistake of relying too much on Amazon's reputation and algorithms to attract customers to their products. After creating their product listings, they just stop there. They don't have a marketing gameplan in place to create buzz towards their products. This is a huge mistake you don't want to make if you really want to be successful on Amazon. In fact, before you even create listings and ship your products, you should already have a marketing game plan in place.

So here's my question for you. What is your Amazon marketing gameplan? If you have one, that's great. If you don't have one, don't worry, I'll provide you with a practical framework for one. When you create a gameplan, you merely think of the ways on how you can direct attention towards your products. You don't have to be a marketing genius to come up with an actionable marketing plan for your Amazon business. Here's an overview of the marketing strategies you should include in your marketing gameplan:

1. Optimize your listings with search engine optimization (SEO). I touched on this topic earlier in this chapter. Just like most online marketplaces, Amazon makes use of algorithms to help

consumers find products on their platform. This algorithm takes a look at the relevant keywords used in the creation of a product listing and use these as basis in determining what the product is all about and to whom they should recommend it to. If a listing contains the keywords soccer memorabilia, then Amazon would recommend the product to Amazon shoppers who search for soccer memorabilia.

2. Purchase sponsored ads for your product listings on Amazon. Yes, I know, this is going to cost you a considerable amount of money but I assure you that the return on your investments is completely worth it if you buy ads properly. Buying sponsored ads within Amazon is a very practical strategy especially for new sellers who want to jumpstart their sales and reviews. Advertising achieves two very important things. One, it provides your products their much-needed exposure and visibility. And two, advertising is the most effective on-site strategy to increase and drive sales.

The sponsored products and sponsored brands advertising programs by Amazon follow the cost-per-click model. This means that you only pay for your ads when a visitor actually clicks on the ads. You are also always in control of your advertising costs. The program has a reporting and tracking system which enables you to see the progress of your advertising campaign. You can learn what's working for your products and how you can fine-tune your campaigns to further generate better results.

3. Share your product listings on social media. Product listings on Amazon come with their own unique URLs. This means that you can copy the URL links and share them in social media sites that accept link posts (Facebook, Twitter, YouTube, Pinterest, LinkedIn). It's the perfect way to get your product in front of consumers. To get the most out of social media, you should consider

creating pages for your Amazon business. This enables you to build a following for your business. You can promote your products to these loyal customers over and over again.

You can make things even better by purchasing ads in social media to promote your Amazon product listings. This is not against Amazon's policies so you have nothing to be worried about. Almost all of the major social media sites today have their own advertising programs. You should take advantage of these programs to drum up attention for your products. Advertising in social media sites is not as expensive as you might think. For example, you can purchase ads for a few dollars a day on Facebook. For a few dollars a day, you have the potential of reaching thousands if not millions of potential customers.

4. Get in touch and partner with influencers. I will discuss this strategy a little bit in the succeeding chapter (Chapter 8: Strategies on How to Generate Your Initial Product Reviews). The idea behind this strategy is that influencers, which are considered as online celebrities, can help you get the word out about your products. It can generate instant results if the influencer has a huge following online. Needless to say, you should only deal with influencers whose followers are composed of your target market. For example, if you are selling art supplies on Amazon, you should only work with influencers who are in the art niche.

5. Start a blog and use it to drive targeted traffic towards your product listings. This is a no-brainer. Why? There are several reasons why writing a blog can be the best thing you'll ever do for your Amazon business. One, blogs are easier to rank on search engines because of how their contents are updated on a regular basis. Search engines like Google love fresh content and it so happens that blogs are the perfect platforms to publish fresh content. Use the blog to provide additional information about your products that you can't pack in the descriptions of your

listings. There are so many things you can do with the blog to drum up interest for your products. You can create tutorials on how your products are used. You can write articles and guides about the products. And so on and so forth.

6. Get serious with email list building and marketing. If you are selling something online, it's paramount that email marketing is a mainstay in your marketing kit. Almost everyone who uses the internet has an email address. Building an email list is a powerful way to keep your customers loyal. This applies very well with the Amazon FBA program. Your marketing strategy should include creating an email list of the people who are interested in buying your products. If you are launching a new product, you can send out notifications via email about this new product. This is a very effective method. Some online marketers are so successful with email marketing that they get most of their customers from their email lists. I'm not saying that you can accomplish the same thing with your Amazon FBA program but it will surely help you in a significant manner.

Keep implementing these marketing strategies for the whole time that your products are listed on Amazon. Your product is just another product on Amazon if you don't do your marketing right. Keep in mind that there are millions of products on Amazon. Your products are literally floating alongside thousands of competitors and similar products. The only way for you to get ahead of the others is through aggressive marketing campaigns.

Chapter 8: Strategies On How To Generate Your Initial Product Reviews

I'm telling you right now. Gathering reviews for your products is without a doubt one of the most important pieces in the complicated jigsaw puzzle that is the Amazon FBA program. Generally speaking, the more reviews your product gets, the higher it ranks in the search results when a customer searches for products on Amazon. Amazon uses the number of reviews that a product listing gets to gauge the product's popularity and value to customers. Doing the logic, if your product has zero or very little reviews, then Amazon's algorithm can easily decide that your product is next to useless. It's for this very reason that you need reviews for your products, especially if your products are green and newly-listed.

Before you proceed in attracting reviews for your products, you need to be aware that there are certain methods that you can no longer use. Amazon has been more discerning when it comes to reviews posted on the site. There are some methods to attract reviews that used to be accepted by Amazon which are now prohibited. These include the following.

1. Purchasing reviews – This is completely against the terms of Amazon. Buying reviews is strictly prohibited by the retail giant. The company wants to be a fair marketplace and the idea of purchasing reviews is against this goal. People who are paid to leave reviews will surely write positive reviews. After all, they are being paid by the people selling the products they are reviewing. Amazon prohibits this practice and if you are caught doing it, the company could easily terminate your account and even ban you from the site. Being banned on Amazon means you can neither sell nor buy items on the platform.

2. Offering heavy discount codes – In the early days of the Amazon FBA program, most sellers would offer their new products at heavily discounted prices to attract instant customers. Sellers would price their products at 90% off, which basically means they are giving away their goods in exchange for reviews. Amazon has caught on to this tactic, and they have decided to ban it. Sellers aren't allowed to sell products at such very high discount rates in exchange for reviews because the heavy discount can lead to very biased reviews.

3. Using review exchange groups – This is another method that was heavily used to great effect back in the early days of the Amazon FBA program. It's a method that no longer works because Amazon is completely against it. Giving your products away in exchange for a review is no longer a viable strategy. Another reason this method no longer works is the fact that Amazon is getting better in detecting, flagging, and deleting reviews that were left behind by people who received the products for free.

Stay away from these old and prohibited methods of generating reviews for your products on Amazon. If you are caught engaging in these activities, Amazon can ban your account and prohibit you from joining their program again. You must always comply with the community guidelines if you want to last long in the program.

Rules by Amazon When It Comes to Generating Product Reviews

1. Don't offer a voucher or a free gift in exchange for product reviews. This is a form of incentivizing a review. Amazon doesn't allow reviews that are posted in exchange for compensation of any kind (i.e. cash payments, discounts on future purchases, entry to a competition or prize raffle, free product, reimbursements, and refunds).

2. You are not allowed to write reviews for your own products. You are not even allowed to use as description your own reviews of the product. If you want to review your products for your target audience, publish your reviews in a separate platform like a blog, website, or forum.

3. You are also not allowed to write reviews about products being sold by your competitors. It's not an equal playing field if you are writing reviews about competitor products because there will always be bias in your reviews. It's for this reason that you are not allowed to review products by your direct competitors.

4. You can ask your buyers to leave reviews provided that you don't specifically tell them to leave a "positive" review. For example, you can say "I would appreciate it very much if you could leave a review of the product in my Amazon listing." But you can't say "I would appreciate it very much if you could leave a positive review of the product in my Amazon listing". There's a huge difference between asking for a review and asking for a positive review. When you request for a review, the customer should have the choice to write a negative or a positive review.

5. You can't use a third party service provider that offers discounted or free products in exchange for reviews of your products. For example, you can use a review club to generate reviews for your products.

6. You can't place an insert into the packaging of your products which instructs customers to leave a positive review of your product. You can use an insert that asks customers to leave a review but you can't ask them to specifically write a positive review. Please refer to number four (4) in this list.

Now that you know what to do and what not to do, let us now look into the various strategies that you can effectively implement to generate the initial reviews for your newly listed products on Amazon.

1. Set up an email autoresponder, which automatically sends requests for your customers to write reviews about the products they purchased from you. Most people who shop on Amazon don't bother writing reviews but they will do so if you ask them nicely. And that's the point of setting up an email autoresponder. The good news is that there are applications that you can use to automate this process. A good example of an email autoresponder that you can use for your Amazon FBA business is Feedback Genius. What this application does is send emails to customers who have received your products. It simply asks for a review on your behalf.

To set up the application, you just have to write down a message thanking the customer for the purchase and asking politely if he/she can take the time to write and leave a review. The application automatically changes the names of the recipients. Let's say for example that a woman named Maria bought an item from your Amazon store called Jerry's Apparel. The application can automatically send the following message to her inbox once it is known that Maria has received the product.

Dear Maria,

Hello, I hope you are having a good day. My name is Jerry and I'm the seller behind Jerry's Apparel. This is a family business and I would like to make sure that you have the best experience in shopping with us. First of all, I would like to thank you for buying our products. It's a pleasure doing business with you and I am really hoping that the product arrived at your doorstep on time and that it's everything you expected.

We want to make sure that you are completely satisfied with the sale. With that said, if you don't mind, we would appreciate it very much if you can leave an honest review of the product you received in our Amazon listing. We would like to hear your thoughts about your shopping experience with us so that we can further improve our products and our services.

It will only take a minute or two to leave a review on Amazon. Your feedback about our product and your shopping experience with us is greatly appreciated. Thank you very much and we're looking forward for your honest review.

Sincerely,

Jerry

Asking your customers to leave reviews is a very effective strategy. Put yourself in the shoes of your customers. If you buy something from Amazon, it's most likely that if you receive the item, you never bother leaving a review. But what if you receive a message in your inbox thanking you for your purchase and asking you if you can leave a review? It's something that you feel the need to reply to especially if you are satisfied with the product.

2. Get your friends, family, and colleagues to purchase your product and then leave a review for it. This is the quickest way to start the reviews rolling in. However, you need to instruct them not to purchase the item from the same IP address as you because this can trigger Amazon's algorithm and cause your product listing to be red flagged. Amazon is in a serious campaign to weed out artificial reviews in its system because these are deemed as detrimental to the experience of shoppers in the site.

Amazon will remove reviews if they learn that there is a very close connection between the owner of the products and the reviewer. For instance, if Amazon learns that the person who left a review for your product is your sibling, that review will likely be deleted. You can get around this by making sure that Amazon can't make out the connection between you and the reviewer. This is why I've mentioned above the importance of telling your friends and family to purchase your product and leave reviews using unique IP addresses. This way, Amazon's algorithm won't be able to figure out the close connections you have with the reviewers.

3. Get in touch with online influencers whose niches are relevant to the products you are selling. Influencers are basically people who have considerable numbers of following online, mostly through blogs or through social media sites like Facebook, Instagram, and Twitter. They are sometimes referred to as internet celebrities. You can use them as leverage to jumpstart the sales as well as the reviews for your products being sold on Amazon. What you need to do is find influencers whose audiences might be interested in your products.

For example, let's say that you are selling makeup kits on Amazon. After launching your products, you look for influencers in the beauty niche and ask them if they are interested in promoting your products. Of course, there will be some sort of payment here. How much you pay the influencer depends on how popular he/she is. The deal usually goes this way: you send your product to the influencer, she reviews it, she recommends it to her fans, and you pay her for her efforts. This is a very powerful way to generate initial reviews for your products because all of the incoming reviews are organic. These are the types of reviews that Amazon prefers.

4. Take advantage of the Amazon Early Reviewer Program. Amazon announced this program just around the time they started prohibiting incentivized reviews on the site. This program basically enables selected groups of customers to write reviews for products that are enrolled in the program. Customers who leave reviews are paid by Amazon with credits of $1 to $3. However, enrolling your product in the Early Reviewer Program is going to cost you $60. You will pay this amount when you get your first review.

Is $60 too much to pay for product reviews especially if you are only earning a few bucks from every sale you make? I would say it's worth it if you are new in the business and you want to attract reviews to jumpstart your product's presence on Amazon. Never lose sight of the fact that products with lots of reviews are highlighted more often on the site. More reviews lead to more sales. It's a snowball effect, so to speak. There are some requirements before you are eligible to enroll a product in the Early Reviewer Program. The product should have less than five reviews and its selling price must be beyond $15.

5. Make use of product inserts. Inserts are printed messages that are added inside the packaging of your products. You can put whatever information or instructions you want in these inserts. You can put information about your blog or your social media pages. You can put information on how the customer can contact you. And of course, you can put instructions requesting customers to write reviews for the product on Amazon. This is not in violation of Amazon's ban on incentivized reviews. You are simply asking your customers to leave reviews if they are interested in doing so.

Take the time to design an insert that's both catchy and appealing. You might want to hire a graphics designer to get it done for you. The goal is to make the insert appealing enough so that the customer will take notice of it and actually read it and not just throw it away. Some sellers use practical inserts that the customer can reuse like bookmarks or greeting cards.

6. Offer your products at discounted prices. You have to be careful with this strategy because you might get flagged for incentivized reviews. The general rule is that your discounts for products, especially newly launched products, should not exceed 50%. Discounts that are beyond this threshold is often taken by Amazon as a red flag because it suggests that you are driving your prices down with the goal of getting reviews. To avoid this problem, you should offer normal discount rates. It should be between 5% and 25%. Your listing is less likely to be flagged because there are millions of products in the Amazon marketplace that offer discounts in the 5% to 25% range.

7. When launching a new product, simultaneously launch it to a targeted email list. This is very similar to what I've discussed on the number one strategy in this list. Of course, this assumes that you already have an email list. This strategy accomplishes two very important things. First, the initial sales jumpstart your products on Amazon which also means you could get a few reviews right off the bat. And second, you are actively building a list of loyal customers. You are hitting two birds with one stone. You are making sales and you are building your list.

8. Make the most of customer services. Have you ever experienced getting amazing services from a business that you feel obligated to provide them with a nice review? Online shoppers experience the same thing. If you are a seller and you always go beyond in ensuring that your customers receive the highest-quality products and services, your customers are more likely to leave a positive review of your products.

These strategies are not that difficult to implement. They are very practical and anyone can do them. I suggest that you use every single one of them if you want to maximize the number of reviews that you can potentially generate.

Chapter 9: How To Use As Leverage The Amazon Sponsored Products Feature

Amazon offers its sellers three advertising solutions: Sponsored Products, Sponsored Brands, and Stores. If you are a small or medium-sized seller on the Amazon FBA program, your best option is the Sponsored Products feature which is going to be the sole topic in this chapter. Sponsored Products is described by Amazon as "ads for individual product listings on Amazon." The company adds that these advertisements "appear on search results pages and product details, helping drive sales and product visibility". In other words, if you want your product listings to be seen by more people on Amazon, you should absolutely take advantage of the Sponsored Products feature.

The Sponsored Products feature follows the cost per click or pay per click model. This means that you only pay for clicks that your ads generate. If a lot of people view the ads but they don't click on it, then you don't have to pay anything. Again, you only pay for clicks registered by the system. How much you pay per click depends on various factors. The biggest factor is of course the competition for the ads. When you create an ad on Amazon, you are basically bidding for certain keywords and placements. You are competing with other advertisers. The tougher the competition, the higher you have to bid for your ads.

In a nutshell, how much you pay per click isn't fixed. However, you have full control over how much you want to spend on your ads. You identify a maximum bid which means Amazon won't charge you more than your maximum bid. In most cases, the amount you pay for each click that your ad gets is usually lower than your cost per click bids. Nevertheless, you should not bid more than you are willing to pay for an ad click. This ensures that you are always operating within you advertising budget.

Reasons You Should Use the Amazon Sponsored Products Feature

1. It can significantly increase the visibility and sales of your products. Here's what happens when you get an ad on Amazon. When a consumer searches on Amazon for a product and it happens that the search term is relevant to your product, your product listing will appear in the search results. This means that even if your listing doesn't have a rank when it comes to sales and reviews, it still has the chance to appear in the top results. In a sense, getting an ad evens the playing field for you. Not only will your ad appear in the search results, it can also appear in the details pages of other products. For example, if you are selling a laptop, your ad for the laptop can potentially appear in a page for another laptop. The sponsored product ads usually appear below the images for the product in the listing.

2. The sponsored products feature doesn't have a monthly fee. As we have mentioned earlier in this chapter, the program follows the cost per click model. You only pay when a shopper on Amazon clicks on one of your ads. If the shopper clicks on the ad, he will be redirected to your own product listing. You only pay for the click when the redirection is completed and recorded by the advertising program's trackers.

3. You are in full control of your advertising budget. Because you only pay when your ads are clicked on, you control your expenses by managing the maximum bids you are willing to pay for each click. It's impossible for your expenses to go beyond what you have budgeted for the ad campaign. You can terminate any active ad campaign anytime you want. You can also customize and update the ads for better results.

4. Sponsored ads can appear in desktop browsers and mobile browsers. This is very important because a growing percentage of Amazon shoppers are accessing the website through their smartphones and other small-screen devices. Your ads can also appear in the Amazon mobile app. In short, the Sponsored Products feature takes your product listings everywhere. This translates to more eyeballs, more customers, and more sales.

5. The minimum daily budget is only $1. That's right. You can run an advertising campaign on Amazon with just a daily budget of $1. However, this small budget is only advisable for very small niches wherein there's very little competition. If you want to really reach a lot of customers, your daily budget should be at least $10. A minimum of $10 a day ensures that your advertising campaigns run throughout the day. You see, if you set a budget that's below $10, your budget can run out before the day has ended.

6. It's a very powerful tool especially if you are trying to sell seasonal items. Let's say for example that Christmas is around the corner and you are selling Christmas sweaters. There are hundreds of Christmas sweaters beings sold on Amazon. It will be next to impossible to get your product listing to rank high in the search results. The only way to make sure that your listings are seen by people is to purchase sponsored ads on the site. The sponsored ads enable you to boost the visibility of your time-sensitive products on the site. It's an effective strategy in boosting sales for seasonal items.

7. It enables you to clear out products that you want to phase out of your listings. If there are items in your listings that aren't doing very well and you want to change them or get rid of them altogether, purchasing ads for these listings can make the process a lot easier. By promoting

these goods through sponsored ads, you give them a better chance of being seen by people. If you want to run a successful clearance sale, purchasing sponsored ads is one of the ways to do it.

8. Sponsored ads help spark interest for your new products. Shoppers can't buy products that they aren't aware of right? That's what sponsored ads bring to the table. They bring awareness for your new products. You see, when you create a new product listing, it can be slow for the product to gain views and sales. We are talking about weeks and months here. Sometimes, a year passes by and a product is yet to generate a sale. This is all too common on Amazon. The main culprit for this problem is it's not that the product is bad, it's just that nobody knows about it yet. You have to build awareness for it first before it can start generating sales. To fast-track the build-up of awareness for the product, you should purchase a sponsored ad for it.

9. The Sponsored Products program comes with tracking and reporting features that can help sellers understand how consumers are interacting with their product listings. There's a ton of valuable information that you can gather from these ad tracking reports. You can learn what kinds of keywords are attracting the most clicks. You can identify which products listings are getting the most views. You then use these new information to further improve the look and contents of your product listings.

10. Sponsored ads directly send people who click on the ads to your product listing. Your product detail page is the landing page. The customer doesn't have to go through hoops to get to your offer. With just one click, the customer is on your product details page.

How to Create a Sponsored Products Ad

On the main dashboard of your Amazon Seller account, go to the Advertising tab and click on Campaign Manager. From here, just follow the instructions and fill up the necessary information. The steps are not that difficult to follow. Give your ad campaign a name, set your daily budget, and enter the duration of the campaign. After completing this, you then choose your targeting method. You have two options with regards to targeting. You can pick your own keywords through manual targeting or you can let Amazon choose the keywords for you through automatic targeting.

After choosing your targeting type, the next step is to select the items from your current product listings that you want to advertise. Amazon encourages you to organize these listings into ad groups. You are allowed to create several ad groups within a single campaign. With the ad groups in place, you now select how much you are going to bid for the ads. You will be provided with a list of suggested keywords to bid on. Choose the ones you want to bid or you can manually add the keywords you want to target. There's a separate bid for each keyword.

That's it. Just click on the button that says "save and finish" and your ad will go live in a short while. To check if your ad is live and active, just go back to the Campaign Manager window and look at the list of ad campaigns that are marked as active.

Tips and Best Practices in Using the Sponsored Products Feature

1. Before you run an advertising campaign, make sure that you have clear goals in mind. Your goals will shape your advertising strategy. For example, if generating sales is your priority, then your focus should be on converting clicks into orders. To see if you can reach your sales goals, you have to track your advertising cost of sale which is calculated by dividing your advertising

costs over your total sales from advertising. This helps you determine if your advertising campaigns are returning your investments.

2. Choose the right products to advertise. First of all, make sure that your products are in stock. They must also be priced competitively so that consumers will have an easier time noticing them. If your advertised products are priced too high compared to the competition, consumers will rarely check you out. If your advertised products are priced too low compared to the competition, consumers will assume that you are offering low-quality products, thus the low prices. With that said, you need to find price points that hover within the price ranges of your competitors.

3. The details in your product listing should be complete. Incomplete listings with very little information look amateurish and untrustworthy. The general rule is that every piece of information the customer needs to know about the item should be provided in the description of the listing. Amazon specifically names five criteria that the listing must have. These are as follows:

- Accurate and descriptive titles
- Relevant and useful product information
- High quality product images
- At least five (5) bullet points
- Hidden keywords

4. You need to set a daily budget that should be enough to keep your ad running for the duration of the day. The problem with using a very small budget is that there is the chance that it runs out in the middle of the day. If this happens, your ads will immediately showing up in the search

results. Because of this, you might miss out on potential ad impressions and clicks. Although the minimum daily budget for sponsored products ads on Amazon is $1, it's still best that you use a higher budget. Start with at least $10 a day. This should be more than enough to keep your ads running for a whole day.

5. It's best that you always keep the ads active to maximize their exposure. When you create an ad, you have the option of setting an end date for the ad or you can set it to keep on running as long as there's a budget in your account. We highly recommend that you don't put an end date so that the ad will keep running. This helps consumers find your products any time they search on Amazon. This is a good strategy to keep improving the demand for your products.

6. Try automatic targeting when choosing the type of targeting for your ads. With automatic targeting, you let Amazon choose the keywords and do the work of matching your ads to the terms that customers use to search on the site. Amazon uses its algorithm to choose the best keywords and matches for your ads. And of course, there's the added benefit of saving time on your part because the targeting will be done by the company, not by you. Furthermore, with automatic targeting, the keywords in your ads are regularly updated depending on changes in Amazon search trends.

7. Learn how to bid competitively. A lot of sellers on Amazon often make the mistake of bidding too low for their ads because they think they are saving money. That is never the case. As you lower your bidding, you are actually decreasing the ROI (return on investment) in your ads. Lower bids will lead to lesser visibility and decreases sales. This is especially true if your products belong to a really competitive niche. With many sellers bidding for the same keywords as yours, you will be left behind if you don't bid as much as they bid.

8. Make it a point to check the reports on the performances of your ads. You can access these tracking reports in your dashboard. There are so many things you can learn from the data contained in these reports. You can draw conclusions from the data which you will then use to further improve future versions of your ads. The reason why these reports exist is so that you can learn from them and improve your ad campaigns.

9. Try A/B testing sponsored products. A/B testing is a marketing strategy that involves running two similar ads at the same time with the goal of determining which type of ads will generate the best results. For example, you get two sponsored product ads for two very similar items in your inventory. You let the ads run for the same period then track their performances. At the end of the testing, you should be able to pinpoint which ad performed better. You move forward by using that type of ad more often in your succeeding ad campaigns. As for the slow-performing ad, either you deactivate it or you improve it with the hope of generating better results.

10. Target at least thirty (30) keywords in your sponsored products advertising campaigns. This sounds like it's too much but it's not. Just think of the terms and phrases that your target customers may use in searching for your product on Amazon. Various combinations of these terms and keywords can be in the hundreds. So it's completely rational and practical to target at least thirty keywords in your ad campaigns. To find relevant keywords for your main keywords, you can use external keyword research tools like Google's own keyword planner. The Google keyword planner is free to use. Just log in with your Gmail account.

11. Write detailed titles for your product listings. This is a no-brainer but a lot of Amazon sellers still take it for granted. When a person searches for items on Amazon, the first thing that he

reads is the title of the listing. It should be descriptive so that the customer will know what the product is all about without scrolling down. Remember that your ads will be appearing alongside dozens of other products. If your title is not descriptive enough, it will be difficult for it to catch the attention of the consumer.

12. Product images are also very important. Online shoppers are known for judging products based on the images that come along with the product listings. With that said, you should take extra efforts in taking high quality photos that you are going to use in your listings. Create professional lighting and solid backdrops if you have to. You can achieve these with just a simple digital camera. Photos taken with digital cameras really translate well when uploaded online so you have nothing to be worried about. As much as possible, you should take full photos of the items you are selling with a white background. Take separate photos of parts or detachable items if necessary. You can upload several photos with every product listing you make.

The main gist of this chapter is that if you want to maximize your product's visibility on Amazon, you should set aside a budget for advertising campaigns through the Sponsored Products feature. It's a strategy that will reward you both in the short-term and in the long-term.

Chapter 10: Practical Tips On How To Attract More Customers For Your Amazon Products

We have discussed some of the most technical aspects of starting an Amazon FBA business in the previous chapters. In this chapter and in the next two chapters, we are going to discuss how to actually run and manage the business side of the venture. Selling products through the FBA program is a business no matter how much time you put into it. Whether you do it part-time or full-time, you have to seriously treat it as a business if you want to generate any revenue from your efforts.

For this chapter, we are going to cover the various strategies that you can implement to attract more customers to your business. These are methods that thousands of Amazon sellers use to double or even triple their revenues from Amazon. I've used all of these methods myself and they've helped me greatly in achieving success on the Amazon platform.

1. Regularly offer discounts. Discounts are among the cornerstones of effective retail marketing. Consumers are always looking for items that they can purchase at lower costs. They are hardwired to purchase items being offered at discounted prices because they are afraid of missing out. Countless studies have shown over and over again that a person is more likely to buy an item if there's a discount being offered no matter how small that discount is. What's great about Amazon is that you can create your discount rates right off the bat. This means that even if you have just created the product listing, you can sell the item at a discounted price.

2. Set up a blog with the goal of using it to drive external traffic to your product listings. If you are going to follow this strategy, be ready to be in it in the long run because it takes time for a blog to grow its readership. It also takes time for the search engines to index the contents of the blog and rank its pages in their search results. Blogging is a very powerful tool especially if you have good writing skills. Your blogging strategy should involve creating valuable content that are relevant to the products you are selling on Amazon. This way you could subtly promote your Amazon products in relation to your blog content without sounding too salesy.

3. Build an email list. We have touched on this topic quite a few times in previous chapters. It's referred to by many names. Sometimes it's called email marketing, list building, email list building, and newsletter marketing. How email marketing works is simple. You collect email addresses from your target customers and put them in an email list. You can market to this email list whenever you have a new product or you have important updates that your email subscribers might be interested in. An email list allows you to nurture a loyal customer base. As long as you keep providing them with high quality and valuable products, they will be supporting you down the road. That's the end goal of email marketing. It matches perfectly well with the Amazon FBA program.

4. Collaborate with other Amazon sellers. Yes, you can work together with other sellers on Amazon, even the ones that are technically your competitors. The goal in collaborating with other sellers is to use each other's clout as leverage in promoting each other's products. This can't be done on the Amazon website itself so you have to collaborate outside of the platform. For example, you can promote each other's products on your blogs or social media pages. If you are wondering, this type of collaboration is not against any of Amazon's rules and policies. You are simply promoting each other's goods.

5. Partner with influencers. This is another method that we have touched on quite a few times in previous chapters so you already have an idea as to how it works. Customers are more likely to buy products that are recommended by people who are knowledgeable about the products. For instance, a woman looking for a lipstick is more likely to purchase a lipstick if it's recommended by a beauty blogger. What you do is look for influencers in your niche whom you can tap to recommend or mention your products to their followers and fans. These influencers can be bloggers, vloggers, or social media celebrities.

6. Engage in content marketing. Content marketing is the technique of creating content and distributing these in various external platforms with the goal of building awareness about your products. These pieces of content you distribute online should contain a link back to your own blog, website, or even directly to your product listing. This is a great method of creating instant buzz around your products. If you have a lot of friends and contacts in your niche who are more than willing to publish your content in their own platforms, content marketing can be a great source of consistent traffic for your website, blog, and product listings.

7. Advertise your products on social media networks. All of the major social networking sites today have their own advertising programs. You can purchase ads in Facebook, Twitter, Instagram, YouTube, LinkedIn, and even Pinterest. It's not that expensive to buy ads from these platforms. They are actually cheap compared to other forms of online advertising. For example, you can run an ad on Facebook for one week with a budget of $50 to $100. This ad has the potential to reach thousands if not hundreds of thousands of potential customers. The same can be said about the advertising programs of Twitter, Instagram, and LinkedIn. You should take

advantage of these advertising programs to maximize the online visibility of your Amazon products.

8. Advertise your Amazon products using external advertising programs. Aside from Amazon's own Sponsored Products feature and social media advertising, you should also consider purchasing ads from online ad programs like Google Ads. Google Ads is the largest ad provider online so you should start with it. A lot of sellers on Amazon purchase ads that send people to their websites or blogs. They then refer these visitors to their product listings on Amazon. In essence, it's a two-step process. You get ads to promote your blog then you use the blog send visitors to your Amazon listings.

9. Think globally. Look for products that can be shipped for an international market. Offering your products to a global market is one of the keys to increasing your sales. Why limit yourself to the North American market when you can offer your products for interested customers in Europe, Australia, and even Asia.

You should have realized by now that online marketing can be very time-consuming. There are so many things that you can do but you only have very little time. That said, I am not in any way saying that you should utilize all of the marketing strategies I have discussed in this chapter. There will be too much in your plate if you attempt to use them all at the same time. What I would suggest that you do is experiment with them in batches then track the results you are getting from them.

Find the strategies that get you the most results and stick to them. Make these strategies your priority in your marketing campaigns. This doesn't necessarily mean that you ditch the strategies that generated the least results for your business. Try experimenting with them whenever you can. You might generate better results the second time or third time around. All of these methods work if you implement them right.

Chapter 11: Common Pitfalls And Mistakes You Should Avoid When Selling On Amazon FBA

There is no guarantee that you will be successful selling products through the Amazon FBA program. I am not trying to discourage you, I am merely telling you the reality. The truth is that a large percentage of those who try the program don't make any money at all. However, you can take comfort in the fact that most of these people fail because they didn't do the right things. They made too many mistakes that led to their failure on the platform. So in this chapter, we are going to look into the most common pitfalls and mistakes that new sellers make on Amazon.

Try to avoid making these mistakes at all costs.

1. Incomplete or incorrect product information and description. This problem is more rampant than you think. For online shoppers, there's nothing more frustrating than coming across an Amazon product listing that contains incomplete and erroneous information. It's a huge turn off. Put yourself in the shoes of the customer. Why would you buy a product if the seller can't even get the product data right? Customers would like to know everything they can about a product. If you don't give them the information they are looking for, they aren't going to buy from you.

2. Not reading the rules and policies. Amazon can terminate your Amazon FBA account any time. This has happened to hundreds of sellers. It can also happen to you. The number one reason why this happens is that the sellers break one too many rules and policies. If you break one rule, Amazon might give you a pass. But if you break two or three rules, your account will

likely get terminated. Of course, this all depends on the gravity of your infractions. The only way to avoid this from happening to you is to read the rules, policies, and guidelines put forth by Amazon for their FBA program before you start selling on their platform.

3. Not performing product research. Here's a quick piece of trivia to give you an idea how huge Amazon is. There are 600 million products being sold on Amazon right now. So whatever product you want to sell on the platform, there will always be thousands of competitors you must contend with. If you don't perform you research before selling there, you might get into a niche that is too competitive that it will almost be impossible to make a sale. Product research enables you to identify products and niches that are less competitive which means you have a chance of actually making money off them.

4. Ignoring the importance of keywords in product listings. It's frustrating to think that many Amazon sellers still make this mistake. Keywords are basically the lifeblood of your product listings. If you use the wrong keywords or if you don't use keywords at all, it will be very difficult for consumers to find your products on Amazon. Because you didn't use keywords. Amazon's algorithms will also not be able to identify what your products are and what niches they belong to. Using keywords in your product listings on Amazon is similar to using tags for videos on YouTube. The tags help people find your videos on YouTube. The keywords help people find your products on Amazon.

5. Miscalculating product pricing. Putting a price on your products is one of the most challenging aspects of selling on the Amazon FBA program. You have to do a lot of calculations to ensure that you make a tidy profit from your sales. You need to create a balance between making good profit margins and satisfying your customers with affordable prices. If you price

your product too low, Amazon will eat away at your profit margins. If you price your products too high, you will drive away your customers. That said, you need to master the art of balancing price and customer satisfaction.

6. Forgetting to collect sales taxes. This is a serious matter especially if you are based in the United States. A practical tip I can provide you is that you should fill out your tax settings the day you set up your Amazon account. You can find the Tax Settings section in the dashboard of your Amazon Seller account. It's better to complete the tax settings before you even make a sale. You have the option to pay a fee and allow Amazon to collect the sales tax on your sales. However, the burden of remitting the money to the IRS is still on you. If you are not that familiar with taxation rules and laws especially for online sales, you should consider consulting with a taxation professional.

7. Shipping products to Amazon's fulfillment centers without following Amazon's preparation requirements. If you don't follow Amazon's packaging and preparation requirements, they can refuse your items, return them to you, and repackage them but you will have to pay for the additional costs. If you had serious infractions, they can choose not to deal with you anymore. That's right. They can terminate your account and now allow you to sell on the Amazon FBA program again.

8. Not responding to customer inquiries. When a customer sends an inquiry, you have around 24 hours to respond to the inquiry. If you don't answer the inquiry within the 24-hour period, you will be notified by Amazon. If Amazon notifies you one too many times about these inquiries but you still don't address them, they can suspend your account. Customer support is a very important aspect of selling products on the Amazon FBA program. If you offer fast customer

support, your customers will be more likely to leave you positive reviews. And we all know that positive reviews help in improving the visibility of your product listings on the Amazon search results.

9. Negative interactions with customers. Arguing and debating with customers is a recipe for disaster. Whether you are addressing a happy or an angry customer, you should deal with him in a level-headed manner. If you lose your bearings and start arguing with him, he might leave a negative review for your product. That's a double whammy for you. Not only did you get a headache for arguing with the customer, you also receive a negative review on Amazon. Needless to say, always be positive when interacting with customers.

10. Using product titles that are difficult to understand. Have you come across product titles on Amazon that contain HTML codes, unnecessary symbols, and words that are in CAPS? They are ugly to look at aren't they? When a customer is browsing on Amazon, the first thing he reads about a product is the title. It should be simple, short, and straight to the point. The general rule is that you should keep the title at a maximum of 100 characters. Beyond 100 characters is already too long. Try adding an important keyword or two in the title.

11. Copying product information from other sellers. Not only is this unethical, it can lead to a lot of problems. Even if you are selling similar products with the competitors you are copying from, the details of your items may have significant differences from them. The general rule is that you should never copy the product details and descriptions of other sellers. You should write the descriptions yourself.

12. Not checking the quality of your products before shipping these to fulfillment centers. You should always check and review your products before you prepare, package, and ship them to Amazon's fulfillment centers. Make sure that the products sent to you are in accordance with the deals you have entered into with your suppliers and manufacturers.

These pitfalls and mistakes are too common among new sellers on the Amazon FBA program. Read and understand them carefully so that you won't make the same mistakes. Committing one or two of these mistakes can be disastrous to your Amazon business. For example, not preparing your products properly can get your account suspended.

Chapter 12: How To Effectively Scale Your Amazon FBA Business

Once you start making good money from your Amazon FBA business, the next obvious step is to try scaling your business. It's time to take your business to the next level. The question is, how can you scale your business without significantly increasing your workload? There are several ways on how to accomplish this. It takes a little bit of extra work but it can be done.

Launch More Products

This is the most obvious and most practical scaling strategy. Look for products that you can add to your existing listings. These products should be within the same niche and category as the other products you are selling. For ideas, there are places you can look at like the sub-categories under the current products you have, the sponsored items that appear alongside your product listings, and the recommendations for customers who have bought items from you. Just browse through the products and pick the ones that you can add to your inventory.

Expand Into Additional Markets

I am assuming that your main target markets are North American territories like the United States and Canada. You should consider expanding your offerings to other markets in other countries and regions (i.e. Germany, Japan, United Kingdom, and Australia). For the last several years, Amazon has been building warehouses and fulfillment centers in various international regions. Since a lot of these are new markets, it means that the competition among sellers is not that tough. The earlier you get into these new markets, the more profitable your business will be.

Combine Business Models

You can incorporate multiple business models into your Amazon FBA operations. You don't have to do these within the Amazon platform. You can integrate the other business models externally. For example, you can build a separate online store where you feature and highlight the products you have on Amazon.

As you can see, your options in scaling your Amazon FBA business are quite limited. However, this doesn't mean that there's also a limit to your earning potential. The number of scaling opportunities does not affect the earning potentials of these business models. You can try all three of these methods if you want. You can even implement them at the same time. You can simultaneously launch new products, expand into new markets, and incorporate other business models into your operations.

Conclusion

First of all, congratulations for reading this book up to this point. If you've read and understood every chapter in this book, then you are more than equipped to achieve success on the Amazon FBA program. In the end, your ability to earn any money from the program all comes down to the effort you put into it based on the knowledge you have about selling on the platform. The more you know when you start, the better chances you have in achieving your sales and revenue goals.

But then again, I have to remind you that there's no such thing as "easy money" on the Amazon FBA program. Don't get caught up in the lies and misleading information you can find online about making a quick buck on Amazon. It's definitely possible but it's never sustainable. If you want to build an Amazon business that consistently brings in revenue long-term, then you have to be patient. Focus on searching for high-quality products and promoting them in every marketing channel you can find. High quality products plus effective marketing leads to profits. That's the equation to being successful on Amazon.

All the basic information you need to start selling on Amazon using the FBA program have been discussed in this book. If you ever get confused with something, you can always reread the specific chapter where it was discussed. I would recommend that you always keep a copy of this book in your files so you can easily access it. Some of the chapters take a few readings before you can completely grasp what we've been talking about.

Another important thing I would like to remind you before you start building your Amazon business is that you are going to encounter problems in one way or another. Most of these issues can hit you when you least expect them. For example, a supplier may send you the wrong products or send you the products late. Or a fulfillment center might not accept your shipments because these did not adhere to the rules and policies. Or you miscalculate your pricing and you end up losing money despite a lot of sales. The point here is that anything can happen. You will be facing problems every step of the way.

The trick is to not allow these problems discourage you from pursuing your goals. If you are confident about the quality of your products and your marketing skills, then there's no reason why you should stop. Just keep doing the right things to make sure that you are always in the proper direction. Having problems is part of running an online business.

And last but not the least, make sure to take things in stride. Always be patient. Don't rush things. Don't expect to be making thousands of sales in your first weeks or months. It takes time to build a customer base. You have to remember that consumers are usually wary of new sellers online and they are right for being skeptical.

With that said and done, good luck with your online journey. Follow the advice and strategies I've discussed in this book and you will be in good hands. If you make mistakes, learn from them. If you come across problems, don't let them bog you down. Instead, use them to further improve your products and business.

Printed in Great Britain
by Amazon

47579414R00047